Published by Grolier Books, a division of Grolier
Enterprises Inc.

Disney Presents The Wonderful World of Knowledge
ISBN 0-7172-8929-X
Great Inventions ISBN 0-7172-8946-X

© 1999 Disney

First published in 1999

Printed and bound in China by
Toppan Printing Company

Originated in Italy by Articolor

Designed and compiled by
Marshall Editions Developments Limited

GROLIER
BOOKS

The Wonderful World of Knowledge

GREAT INVENTIONS

Using The Wonderful World of Knowledge

☞**M**ickey, Minnie, Donald, Daisy, Goofy, and Pluto are ready to take you on an adventure ride through the world of learning. Discover the secrets of science, nature, our world, the past, and much more. Climb aboard and enjoy the ride.

Look here for a general summary of the theme

Labels tell you what's happening in the pictures

The Solar System

☞The Solar System is the n given to our Sun and its family planets. It also includes the p moons, millions of pieces of r called asteroids and meteoroi and frozen lumps of dust and called comets. Everything else can see in the sky is outside th Solar System and is far, far away. Every single star is itself a sun, and each may have its own family of planets and moons.

Saturn is surrounded by beautiful rings

Mickey's ears lead you to one of the main topics

The pictures by themselves can tell you a lot, even before you read a word

Watch out for special pages where Mickey takes a close look at some key ideas

REPTILES AND AMPHIBIANS

Color and Camouflage

☞Frogs and toads come in nearly every imaginable color, even gold or black. They have a wide range of patterns, from spots and stripes to zigzags.

Color and pattern help frogs and toads survive. Bright colors warn that they may be poisonous. Drab colors camouflage them, or hide them against their background. Many tree frogs are exactly the same green as leaves, while others look like bark. The Asian horned toad has the best camouflage of all. Folds of patchy, brown skin and a flat body make it look like a dead leaf when it lies still on the forest floor.

Folds of brown skin give perfect camouflage

Flat body is hard to see among dead leaves

Asian horned toad

16

False-eyed frog

Markings look like eyes

For extra protection, bad-smelling liquid oozes out around false eyes

FALSE-EYED FROG
The South American false-eyed frog has large markings on its flanks that look like eyes. These fool some predators into thinking that they are looking at a much larger animal, such as a cat or bird.

COLOR AND CAMOUFLAGE

Dog sniffing curiously at the toad

Oriental fire-bellied toad defending itself against a dog

Skin oozes a stinging fluid

Bright colored belly

STRAWBERRY arrow frog

POISON-DART FROGS
Deadly poison oozes from the skin of Central and South American poison-dart frogs. People in the rain forest rub the tips of their arrows and blowpipe darts on the skin of these frogs to collect the poison to use for hunting.

Blue poison-dart frog

Green and black back

FIRE-BELLIED TOAD
When cornered by a predator, the Oriental fire-bellied toad of eastern Asia arches its back and rears up on its legs to show its fiery underside. Wise attackers back off, because the toad's skin oozes a stinging, bad-tasting fluid.

Toad rears up on its back legs

FIND OUT MORE
MAMMALS: Camouflage
PLANET EARTH: Forests

17

Mickey's page numbers help you look things up. Don't forget there's a glossary and index at the back of each book

Goofy and his friends know how to give you a chuckle on every topic

Mickey points you to more information in other books in your *The Wonderful World of Knowledge*

FIND OUT MORE
MAMMALS: Camouflage
PLANET EARTH: Forests

AMACING FACTS
★ The Sun is enormous compared to the planets. It is nearly 1,000 times more massive than the giant planet Jupiter.

AMAZING FACTS
★ The Sun is enormous compared to the planets. It is nearly 1,000 times more massive than the giant planet Jupiter.

Your favorite characters present some facts to astound you and your friends

THE SOLAR SYSTEM

HOW OUR SOLAR SYSTEM WAS FORMED

1 The Solar System formed 4.6 billion years ago. It started at the center of an enormous swirling cloud of gas and dust.

2 The Sun burst into flames and became a star. Its light and warmth spread throughout the new Solar System.

3 Gas and dust left over from making the Sun clumped together in places. These clumps grew bigger and formed the planets.

4 The planets closest to the Sun are small and made from rock and metal. The larger outer planets are made from gas and liquid.

Numbers lead you step-by-step through how things happen

Pluto is the farthest planet from the Sun

Each planet has its own path, or orbit

Planet orbits

ORBITING THE SUN
No matter how still you try to be, you are always moving. This is because the Earth – and all the other planets – are moving. They are flying through Space around the Sun in looping paths called orbits.

Colorful boxes zoom in on information

Neptune is a cold, blue planet

Uranus is tipped over on its side

THE "PULL" OF GRAVITY
If you throw a ball into the air, it comes down again. The invisible force that pulls it down to Earth is called gravity. The Earth's gravity holds us down on the ground. The Sun's gravity is strong enough to hold all its planets in their orbits.

Gravity pulls a ball to Earth

FIND OUT MORE
PLANET EARTH: Night and day
SCIENCE ALL AROUND US: Gravity

Mars is red and dusty   The Solar System

Mickey's helpers test some ideas themselves

Contents

Great Inventions

Every day someone somewhere thinks of a new idea that improves the way we live, for example a new drug to treat a disease, faster computers to make our work easier, or lighter sportswear to improve our leisure time.

The earliest peoples were just as curious and creative as today's inventors. They had the basic ideas that made all progress possible: tools to light fires for warmth and cooking, plows to prepare the land for farming, and the wheel to move heavy things around.

What is an Invention?

An invention is a new way of making or doing something. Many inventions save time and effort and make life easier. Some inventions improve safety standards. Others just add more fun and enjoyment to life. A discovery is something you find that already exists. People discovered natural fire many thousands of years ago. When they understood how useful fire could be, they invented fire-making tools.

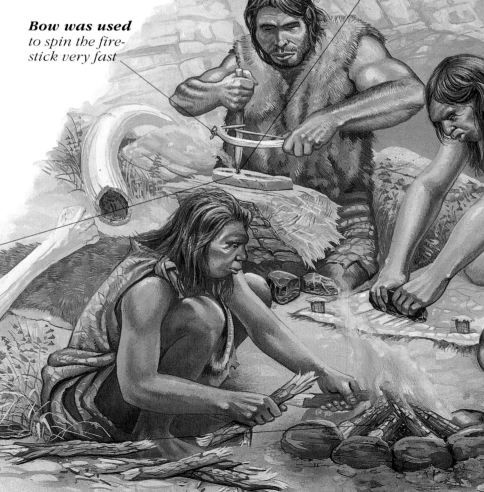

Pointed end of fire-stick fitted in a hole in a flat piece of wood to keep it steady as it spun

Bow was used to spin the fire-stick very fast

RUBBING STICKS

Some inventions help people to survive. Early people discovered that rubbing two pieces of wood together could make sparks to light a fire. To make lighting a fire easier, they made a bow with a string to spin one piece of wood, the fire-stick, very fast against another, flat piece of wood.

Rubbing heated up the two pieces of wood so much that dry bits of grass placed nearby caught fire

Early people making fire

Burning grass was moved to the main fire where it set fire to dry wood

Seat belts are important for road safety

LIFE SAVERS

Many inventions help to save life and protect people from injury. In 1959, a Swedish company fitted the first seat belts inside its cars to keep passengers safe in their seats if the cars crashed. Now, most cars around the world have seat belts.

Two flints, or hard stones, struck against each other also make a spark to light a fire

Early washing machine

TIME SAVERS

The first electric washing machine was made in 1906. Before then, all the laundry had to be washed and rinsed by hand, which took a lot of time and effort. Today, washing machines can wash, rinse, and spin dry our clothes, leaving us time to do other things.

Straws today come in different shapes and are often made of plastic

JUST FOR FUN

Inventions are often popular simply because they are fun. The first paper straws were invented in 1880. They were used as a way of keeping drinks cold (you can suck up your drink without having to touch the glass). People liked using straws to drink, and they have been popular ever since.

FIND OUT MORE
INSIDE MACHINES: Washing machines
SCIENCE ALL AROUND US: Fire

Early Inventions

Early humans lived many thousands of years ago. They discovered fire and invented fire-making tools. These made life more comfortable and led to other inventions, such as lamps and metalwork.

At first, tools were made of hard stones, such as flint. The flint was chipped and shaped into hand axes, which were used to dig holes, cut wood, and kill animals for food. Then, about 8,000 years ago, people discovered that rocks contain metals, such as copper. To remove the metal, the rocks were heated. Then the metal was reheated and shaped into tools, which were stronger than before.

BRONZE TOOLS

About 5,500 years ago, in western Asia, the Mesopotamians learned to mix metals together to make stronger metals. Copper and tin were mixed together to make bronze. The bronze was melted over a fire and poured into shaped molds. This process is known as casting. Once cooled, the metal hardened, making strong weapons and tools.

From c. 3500 B.C., a tool called a crucible was used to pour molten bronze into a mold

Making a stone tool for cutting and scraping

Early people making stone tools and weapons

Ax, with head made from flint, used for cutting wood

Harvesting hook with iron blade and handle made from antler or bone

Flint hand ax

Iron spear for hunting

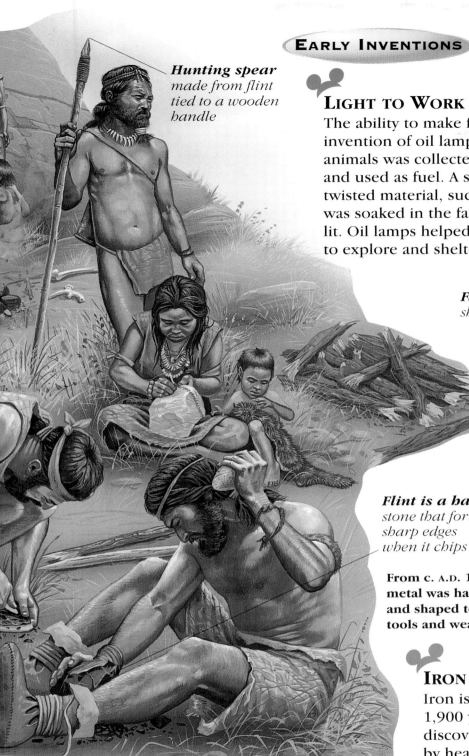

Hunting spear *made from flint tied to a wooden handle*

LIGHT TO WORK BY

The ability to make fire led to the invention of oil lamps. Fat from roasted animals was collected in a rock or shell and used as fuel. A strand of tightly twisted material, such as plant fibers, was soaked in the fat and then lit. Oil lamps helped people to explore and shelter in caves.

Soaked wick *would burn when lit by a flaming twig*

Fat stored in *shell fueled flame*

Shell oil lamp

Flint is a hard *stone that forms sharp edges when it chips*

From c. A.D. 100, hot metal was hammered and shaped to make tools and weapons

IRON TOOLS

Iron is found as an ore in rocks. About 1,900 years ago, people in Mesopotamia discovered that they could remove the iron by heating the ore in a very hot furnace. This process is called smelting. Smelting iron needed more heat than smelting copper, but the iron could make stronger plows and sharp swords.

STONE TOOLS

Making stone tools was skillful, slow work. First, the person had to choose the right kind of stone and then chip it carefully and delicately until it was well shaped, sharp, and comfortable to hold. Modern archeologists have discovered many beautifully made examples of hand axes.

FIND OUT MORE
INSIDE MACHINES: Wedges
PAINTING AND SCULPTURE: Casting

Down on the Farm

Early people were hunter-gatherers, who caught or picked their food. Farming began about 8,000 years ago, when people settled in one place and grew their own food. The invention of the plow and the shaduf helped them prepare and water the land. From that time, farming slowly changed. In the last 300 years, scientific discoveries and new inventions have helped farmers grow bigger and better crops.

TURNING THE SOIL

Wooden plows were used in Ancient Egypt over 5,000 years ago. They were pulled by oxen. Later plows were made of iron, and their shape was changed so that they not only cut the soil, but also lifted it and turned it over. Ox-drawn plows are still used in many countries.

Farmer guided the oxen to make a straight furrow

LIFTING WATER

A 7,000-year-old farm invention, the shaduf, was first used by Ancient Egyptians and is still in use in some countries today. It is a water-lifting lever, with a weight at one end and a bucket at the other.

The shaduf is used to lift buckets of water from a well or stream

Farmer lifted or lowered the arms of the plow to change the depth of the furrow

Plow turned over the soil to prepare the field for seeding

Plowed grooves called furrows

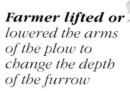

Seeds dropped out through a hole in the bottom of the container

Jethro Tull's seed drill

Horse pulled the seed drill across the field

Team of oxen pulled the plow

BIGGER CROPS

In the 1850s, German and English scientists made studies of plants and developed chemical fertilizers to add to the soil. Later, chemical pesticides to kill off plant pests were also invented so farmers could grow more crops.

Fertilizers improve crop growth

PLANTING SEEDS

In 1701, an English farmer called Jethro Tull invented a seed-sowing machine, named a drill. The seeds were sown in straight, even rows. Farmers were able to weed between the rows using a horse-drawn hoe and to grow more crops.

Plowing a field with an ox-drawn plow

AMAZING FACTS

★ Farmers can now produce huge crops with hydroponics, or the growth of plants using water and nutrients instead of soil. In 1986, 10,000 tomatoes were produced from one plant in just six months.

FIND OUT MORE
INSIDE MACHINES: Levers
STORY OF THE PAST: Farmers

The Wheel

The wheel was invented over 5,000 years ago, and many people believe it is the most important invention there has ever been. By attaching wheels to carts and other land vehicles, it was possible to move people and goods from one place to another. This helped trade to develop. The wheel has also played an important part in engineering and machines, from the early potter's wheel to steam engines, cameras, and clocks.

Early people used *logs or tree trunks to roll a load along*

Mesopotamian *farm cart with solid wheels made from planks*

Egyptian chariot *with two spoked wheels*

Using a potter's wheel in India

WHEELS FROM HISTORY

Before the wheel, people probably used logs to move heavy goods. The first wheels were made from solid planks of wood. Then wheels made with a wooden rim and spokes were lighter and faster. Later, air-filled tires were added to give a more comfortable ride.

Larger, lighter wheels *made coaches in the 1800s easier to pull*

POTTER'S WHEEL

A fast-turning wheel helps potters to shape their clay. The first potter's wheel was used in southwestern Asia in about 3500 B.C.. A kick wheel was added later, which the potter could move with his feet. Modern wheels are driven by electricity.

Tough, air-filled *rubber tires on cars improve grip and help to absorb bumps*

Wheels from early to modern times

Rotating *millstones grind grain into flour*

Grain is *funneled to holes in millstones*

Paddles

Roman waterwheel

Running water *hits the paddles and turns the large wheel*

AMAZING FACTS

★ The wheel as a form of transportation was not used in South America until Europeans took it with them in the 1500s.

GRINDING GRAIN

A waterwheel is a machine that uses the power of water. Its large wheel turns as the flow of water hits the paddles. Waterwheels were invented in Greece, and were used to grind grain into flour for over 2,000 years. Their use soon spread to other areas.

SPINNING WHEEL

Silk has been made in China for centuries. Simple spinning wheels were invented about 3,000 years ago to spin silk, wool, and cotton into a fine, even thread, ready to weave or knit into cloth.

Early Chinese spinning wheel

FIND OUT MORE
STORY OF THE PAST: Wagon trains
TRANSPORT: Cars

Power and Engines

It is hard to believe that up until 300 years ago, work could only be done by people, animals, or the power of wind and water. This changed in the 1700s when the steam engine was invented. The new engine powered transportation and factory machines. The Steam Age continued for 200 years. After that, electricity and gasoline-powered engines took over.

AMAZING FACTS

★ Solar I, in California, U.S., is the world's largest solar power station. It cost $141 million to build in 1982. It uses 1,818 sun-tracking mirrors to produce 10 megawatts of electricity.

STEAMING ALONG

The first steam engines were used to pump water out of mines. In 1763, a Scottish engineer named James Watt was asked to repair a model of one of these engines, but he soon saw a way to improve it. By 1769, he had invented a more efficient steam engine. Watt's invention was such a success that it was used to power machines in factories. His invention also helped other people to develop steam locomotives, or engines, for trains.

Belt wrapped around the flywheel turned the moving parts of other machines

Movement of the piston rocked the connecting rod, which spun the flywheel

Water in a boiler produced steam which forced a piston up and down inside the cylinder

Watt's early steam engine

ELECTRICITY FROM MOVEMENT

In 1869, a French electrical engineer named Zénobe Théophile Gramme invented a dynamo – a machine that changes mechanical movement into electricity – that created a continuous electrical current. Gramme's dynamo produced more electricity than any other dynamo of the time.

Gramme's dynamo

SOLAR POWER

Photoelectric cells turn sunlight into electricity. These cells were invented in Germany in the 1890s. A few, small solar cells will power a pocket calculator. Large panels of cells can be used to provide electricity to people's homes and to power satellites in Space.

Solar energy panels on top of apartments in Tel Aviv, Israel

DRIVING FORCE

Most of the engines inside today's cars are called internal combustion engines. The first one, built in 1859 by the Belgian Etienne Lenoir, was powered by gas. German engineers Gottlieb Daimler and Karl Benz later made gasoline engines that were light enough to power automobiles.

Lenoir's combustion engine

FIND OUT MORE
GREAT LIVES: James Watt
INSIDE MACHINES: Generator

Transportation

People have always tried to travel farther and faster. The Ancient Egyptians added sails to their boats to power them on the Nile. On land, however, for thousands of years the fastest way to travel was by horse. Only with the invention of the steam engine and, later, the gasoline engine was there a real revolution in transportation, with the arrival of trains, cars, and airplanes.

Pilot lay on the lower wings

IN THE AIR

The American brothers Wilbur and Orville Wright built the first powered plane that ever flew. In 1903, their biplane, or double-wing plane, called *Flyer*, managed to take off and stay in the air for just under a minute. Although it was short, the flight was historic and proved it was possible to fly.

Ancient Egyptian boat with sails

ON THE WATER

The first boats with sails appear in Egyptian drawings from about 3500 B.C.. The sails used the power of the wind to drive the boat along. Eventually sailors set out on longer journeys and learned to steer their course using the position of the stars.

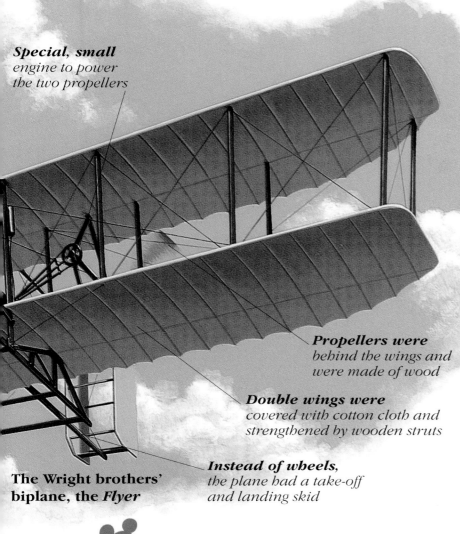

Special, small *engine to power the two propellers*

Propellers were *behind the wings and were made of wood*

Double wings were *covered with cotton cloth and strengthened by wooden struts*

Instead of wheels, *the plane had a take-off and landing skid*

The Wright brothers' biplane, the *Flyer*

ON THE ROAD

The first cars, built by Karl Benz and Gottlieb Daimler, were made in Germany in the 1890s. Known as horseless carriages, these early cars reached speeds of 20 km/h (12½ mph). With no horse to water or feed, travel had become less of a problem.

Gottlieb Daimler in early horseless carriage, c. 1885

ON RAILS

The first steam trains were used to carry coal, but the British engineer George Stephenson proved that they could carry passengers as well. In 1830, he opened the world's first passenger rail line. With the invention of his *Rocket* steam locomotive, rail travel had arrived.

AMAZING FACTS

★ The *Rocket* sped along at 47 km/h (29 mph). This was thought to be so fast that some people feared passengers would suffocate.

Stephenson's *Rocket* engine, pulling a passenger carriage

FIND OUT MORE
INSIDE MACHINES: Airplanes
TRANSPORT: Trains

Space Rockets

For many hundreds of years, space travel was nothing but a fantastic dream. Only the most powerful engine could beat the pull of gravity and leave the Earth behind. One thousand years ago, rockets were little more than fireworks. Since then, scientists have found ways to launch rockets and guide them through Space. This invention has led to a new understanding of the Earth and the exciting exploration of the Solar System.

Rockets shot through the air and exploded into flames

Early Chinese rockets, c. 1200

CHINESE FIRECRACKER

The Chinese experimented with gunpowder from about A.D. 850. At first it was used in fireworks, but later in simple rockets. Exploding gunpowder produced a gas, which shot out of the back of the rockets and forced them through the air like powered arrows. Then they exploded into flames. Europeans later used gunpowder to fire cannonballs.

Handheld launching basket

Sputnik 1 orbiting the Earth

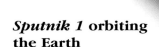

SATELLITE LAUNCH

The Space Age began in 1957 when the former U.S.S.R. launched *Sputnik 1*, the first-ever artificial, or man-made, satellite. Today there are hundreds of satellites in Space. They are used for many different purposes, such as communications and weather forecasting.

AMAZING FACTS

★ *Sputnik 2* launched the first living creature into space – a dog called Laika, who spent a week in orbit in 1957.

Sputnik 1 was *an aluminum ball, only 58 cm (23 in) wide*

ROCKET MISSILE

During the 1930s, German scientists developed the deadly V1 and V2 long-range rocket missiles. These flying bombs bombarded London and other British cities during World War II. Using this rocket technology, scientists eventually produced powerful rockets that transported people into Space.

German V2 rocket, 1942

The satellite weighed *83 kg (183 lb) and carried a radio transmitter*

It stayed in space *for 92 days*

ROCKET POWER

Most early rockets were just simple cylinders made from a variety of materials such as metal, cardboard, and wood. In 1926, American scientist Robert Goddard flew the first liquid-propelled rocket. Using gasoline and liquid oxygen, it only flew for two seconds and reached a height of 12 m (40 ft), but it was an important start.

Robert Goddard with his liquid-fueled rocket

FIND OUT MORE
SCIENCE ALL AROUND US: Fireworks
SPACE: Space travel

New Materials

New materials and inventions go hand in hand. Just as metalworking was a breakthrough for early people, so the discovery of materials such as stainless steel and plastics have brought important changes to modern life.

Every material has its strengths and weaknesses. By combining two materials, scientists can often obtain a mix that contains the strengths of both. New ways of handling old materials may also bring about an invention, such as plate glass. Or scientific invention may result in new materials, such as plastics, which in the last 50 years have replaced many traditional materials.

Most modern toys are made from plastic

NEW STEEL

Stainless steel was developed between 1903 and 1913. A British metal expert, Harry Brearley, discovered that the iron found in steel did not rust in water when a metal called chromium was added to it. This new, stainless, steel was used to make kitchen utensils, which may be washed several times a day.

Stainless steel cooking tools

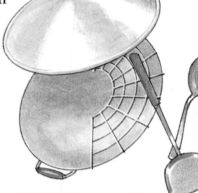

PLASTIC GOODS

The first plastics were made in the 1860s. Modern plastics are light and strong, and will not rot or rust. Objects made from plastic are often cheap. They can be mass-produced in factories, where the plastic is melted and molded into shape.

Plastic for toys and radios can be molded into any shape

Children's toys made from a variety of materials

Before plastics, many toys were made from wood

Refinery processing oil

MADE FROM OIL

During the 1930s, scientists working in oil refineries discovered that some of the chemicals contained in oil could be used to create plastics, such as nylon, and styrofoam.

Plate glass windows on an office building in Tokyo, Japan

NEW WAYS WITH GLASS

For 6,000 years, glass has been made by heating sand with soda and then blowing or molding it. In 1952, a British glassmaker named Alistair Pilkington tried floating melted glass on a huge bath of liquid metal. The cooling glass hardened into large, smooth sheets. This is called plate glass, and it is used in many office windows today.

In the past, dolls were made from china, which broke easily

Tennis racket with a wooden frame, 1880s

BETTER THAN WOOD

In 1968, scientists tried adding strong carbon fiber to plastic. The mix resulted in a new material, which was light and strong. This carbon mix was ideal for tennis racket frames and was soon used instead of wood, which often warped.

Tennis racket with a frame made from a carbon mix, 1980s

FIND OUT MORE
PLANET EARTH: Oil rigs
SCIENCE ALL AROUND US: Materials

Plastic toys are strong, light, and last a long time

Wooden blocks

Big Buildings

People have built big buildings for hundreds of years. Inventions such as pulleys and cranes made it possible to build magnificent temples, huge castles, and towering cathedrals. In 1856, a way of mass-producing steel was developed by removing carbon from iron. Steel is strong and light, and can support a tall building many stories high. The age of the skyscraper had arrived.

AMAZING FACTS

★ The tops of tall skyscrapers sway as much as 1 m (3 ft) on a windy day. People who work in them hear the buildings creak.

SKYSCRAPERS
In 1871, a fire destroyed much of Chicago, U.S.. During the rebuilding of the city, the first skyscrapers were built. These tall buildings had a framework of strong steel beams arranged in a crisscross pattern. Skyscrapers were also built in other cities, where land was expensive.

Floors were held up by a framework of horizontal and vertical beams

Building a skyscraper in New York City, U.S., 1950s

Worker used rivets, or metal pins, to join the framework together

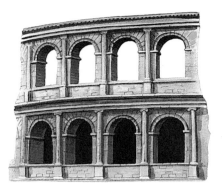

Colosseum, with tiered arches

WIND-PROOF BUILDINGS

Strong winds can make skyscrapers sway. To help prevent this, buildings such as the Citicorp Center in Manhattan, U.S., have heavy weights in their roofs. When the tower sways, a computer tells hydraulic arms to move a platform holding a heavy block of concrete in the other direction. This stops any dangerous swaying.

400-tonne concrete block helps reduce swaying

Construction workers often had to spend the day high above the ground

Steel girders, or beams, were made in many different shapes

ARCHES

Roman builders were the first to put arches to good use. An arch is a way of supporting a building without adding to its weight. The Colosseum, a public arena built in Rome in the first century A.D., has tiers, or levels, of arches on the outside.

Construction of brick and concrete house, showing reinforced rods, Sri Lanka

REINFORCED CONCRETE

In the 1860s, a French gardener found that by adding a wire mesh to wet concrete, he could make stronger flowerpots. In the 1950s, this method was applied to building construction. Nowadays most modern buildings are made using concrete reinforced with steel rods.

FIND OUT MORE
FAMOUS PLACES: Colosseum
INSIDE MACHINES: Hydraulics

Writing and Printing

👉 People have always tried to find ways to communicate. For many years they have used pen and paper to write down and share their ideas. The earliest books were written by hand. This was so slow that books were rare and expensive, and read only by the small number of people who could read or write. The invention of the printing press changed the world. It made books cheaper and more plentiful. This greatly speeded up the spread of knowledge and ideas.

PRINTING PRESS

Early printing was done using carved wooden blocks. By 1452, German goldsmith Johannes Gutenberg was using small metal letters arranged in a wooden frame in a press. They were then inked and pressed against a sheet of paper.

Ancient Chinese papermaking

MAKING PAPER

Paper was invented in about A.D. 105 by Tsai Lun, an official at the Chinese court. He found that mashing woody plants in water and spreading the pulp out to dry made a paper that was both smooth and strong enough to write on. His invention did not reach Europe until over 1,000 years later.

Turning a large screw forced the paper to press on the inked letters

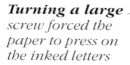
Words were made up from metal letters

Gutenberg's printing press in action

AMAZING FACTS

★ The Ancient Egyptians made ink from squashed beetles.

★ The oldest known printed works were made in Japan around A.D. 764–770.

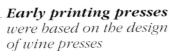

Early printing presses *were based on the design of wine presses*

Printed pages *were hung to dry*

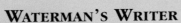

WATERMAN'S WRITER

When Lewis E. Waterman, an American salesman, was about to sign a contract, his pen splashed ink all over the paper. Irritated by this, he invented the first fountain pen in 1884. The pen was designed to allow ink to flow freely and evenly.

Advertisement for Waterman's fountain pen, early 1900s

Felt-tip pens come in many colors

FELT-TIP PEN

Masao Miura and Yukio Horie, from Japan, invented the felt-tip pen with an acrylic tip. It was made in Japan in 1963 and quickly became popular. The pen's soft tip and flowing line made it popular with cartoonists. Others felt that it helped to make their handwriting and drawing lines more graceful, like the brush strokes in Japanese calligraphy.

FIND OUT MORE
COMMUNICATIONS: Printing
INSIDE MACHINES: Screws

Inks were made by mixing *varnish or boiled linseed oil with lampblack, or soot*

Keeping Time

For thousands of years people lived their lives by the Sun. They got up when the Sun rose, ate when it was high in the sky, and slept soon after it set. The first clocks measured time using shadows or the controlled flow of running water or sand. Soon, however, people wanted to divide their day more accurately, and clockmakers began to develop mechanical clocks. These complicated machines led to better timekeeping, as well as the increased understanding of the engineering of moving parts.

MECHANICAL WATER CLOCK

A famous clock built in China in 1088 had a gong to sound the hours. The clock was driven by water power as well as an escapement – a wheel that controlled the speed of the clock's driving force. The clock was housed in a tall tower with a planetarium on the top.

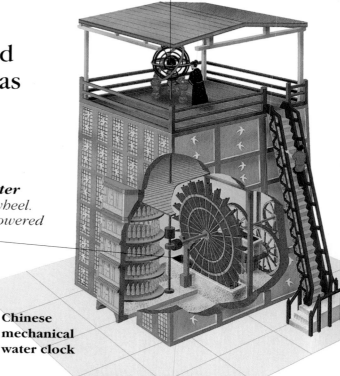

Model of the Solar
System at the top of
the tower

Flow of water
turned the wheel.
The wheel powered
the clock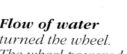

Chinese
mechanical
water clock

SHADOW CLOCK

A moving shadow is one of the oldest ways of measuring time. The Ancient Egyptian shadow clock told the time from markers in the ground. You can see how this worked if you put a stick in the ground on a sunny day and mark the position of its shadow every hour.

You can tell the time
by marking shadow
movement

AMERICAN FACTS

AMAZING FACTS

★ European monks in the 1300s were the first to use alarm clocks. They needed a reliable way of knowing when it was time to get up for morning prayers.

Hands move *around the clock face at a constant speed*

Clock face *has numbers at regular intervals*

Anchor inside allowed *the clock's wheels to move on one cog for each pendulum swing*

Huygens' pendulum clock

PENDULUM CLOCK

The Dutchman Christiaan Huygens was a mathematician and astronomer. In 1656, he made the first pendulum clock. Because his machine was accurate to within about five minutes a day, it had a minute hand, unlike many other clocks of the time.

Heavy weight *pulls the cord, driving the clock's escapement*

Swinging pendulum *rocks the anchor and keeps the clock working*

MAYAN CALENDAR

One of the first accurate calendars was developed by the Mayan people of Central America in about A.D. 500. By observing the Sun, Moon, and stars, Mayan astronomers correctly calculated the length of a month and a year, and even allowed for leap years.

Part of an ancient Mayan stone calendar

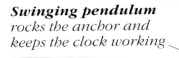

FIND OUT MORE
INSIDE MACHINES: Time machines
SCIENCE ALL AROUND US: Sundial

In the Home

Inventions have helped to improve home life, making it safer, easier, and more enjoyable. In the 1920s and 1930s, electric power started to make many exciting changes. Bright electric lights replaced dim and dangerous gas and oil lamps. New electrical gadgets, such as the hairdryer, saved people time, and the invention of the telephone made it possible to talk to somebody many kilometers away.

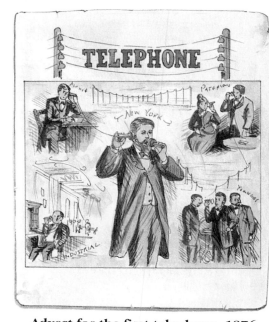

Advert for the first telephone, 1876

RING! RING!

Scotsman Alexander Graham Bell worked in America as a teacher of the deaf. He knew that sounds travel as vibrations in the air. In 1876, he developed the first telephone. It worked by changing sounds into electrical signals that traveled along wires. The telephone at the other end changed them back into sounds.

Inside a hairdryer *is a simple heater and a fan that blows out heated air at high speed*

First handheld hairdryer

Wooden *handle stayed cool*

WASH AND DRY

In the 1920s, an American company made the first hairdryer that you could hold in your hand – the dryer heated up, but the handle did not. Made of wood and aluminum, it was heavier than modern dryers.

AMAZING FACTS

★ Thomas Edison was one of the greatest inventors of all time. Yet he was expelled from school at the age of 12 for being stupid and lazy.

SAFETY MATCHES

The first matches were dangerous to have around the house because they caught fire so easily. Safety matches were developed in the 1850s in Sweden by Johan Lundström. They lit only when struck against the special surface on the book or box.

Early safety matches in a book

LIGHTING THE WAY

Thomas Edison demonstrated the first successful light bulb in America in 1879. He had been searching for something that would glow inside the bulb when electricity passed through it. After trying hair, fishing line, and threads of rubber, cork, and silk, Edison finally succeeded with a carbonized cotton thread.

Edison was responsible for hundreds of scientific developments

Scientists, engineers, and mechanics worked with Edison in his research laboratory

Fine thread with carbon glowed as electricity passed through it

First light bulbs were not very bright

Invention of the first successful light bulb

FIND OUT MORE
COMMUNICATIONS: Telephones
SCIENCE ALL AROUND US: Light bulbs

Food and Drink

People have tried many ways to make fresh food last longer. Drying, salting, and smoking were early ways of treating food to prevent bacteria from spoiling it. However, all these processes affected the food's flavor. In the last 200 years, people have found important new ways of treating and storing food so that it tastes fresh and keeps well. Clever ways of packaging make it easy to take food and drink to work or school, or even into Space.

Canning meat in a food-packaging factory

SEALED CONTAINERS

In 1810, a French candy maker called Nicolas Appert discovered that food that had been heated and sealed in airtight jars stayed fresh for several months. In 1811, two British businessmen used Appert's idea to open a food-packaging factory. Tin cans soon replaced jars – they could be stacked easily and were not breakable.

Canning preserved *food without spoiling its flavor*

Labels were *pasted on the cans*

BEEF

TEA BAGS

In 1908, an American called Thomas Sullivan had the idea of sending samples of tea to his customers in small gauze bags. Each bag contained enough tea for a single cup. Tea bags soon became popular, and making tea became quick and easy – with no messy leaves to throw away.

Drinking tea, New England, U.S., c. 1900

AMAZING FACTS

★ Even though food was first canned in 1811, can openers were not invented until more than 40 years later.

KEEPING COOL

Before the invention of the refrigerator, people had to shop almost daily and keep their food and milk in a cool place, such as a pantry. Between 1913 and 1916, the first electric fridges became available in the U.S..

Refrigerator, 1920s

Vegetables

Dried tomato

Dessert, such as lemon pudding

Astronaut's meal tray

SPACE FOOD

Invented for space travel in the 1960s, food for astronauts is packaged in a tray. The tray can be strapped to an astronaut to stop it from floating away. Most space food is specially dried and needs to have water added to it before it can be eaten.

Large amounts of food were cooked at high temperatures and then canned quickly

Cans were heat-sealed so tightly that a hammer and chisel were needed to open them

FIND OUT MORE
HUMAN BODY: Healthy eating
INSIDE MACHINES: Refrigerator

Good Ideas

Everyone benefits from inventors' ideas. The simplest inventions, from can openers to telescopic fold-away umbrellas, help to make our lives easier. They may also help us to solve some of life's problems simply and quickly.

Inventors get their ideas in different ways. Some inventions are the result of years of hard work and experimentation, while others are the vision of a moment. The invention of Velcro™ was inspired by plants, whereas Post-it™ notes were the result of an accident – an experiment that seemed to go wrong. Some inventions, such as the safety pin, are based on long-forgotten ideas and are reinvented using the materials and technology of a later age.

A telescopic umbrella, which is the same size as a normal one when open, can fit into a bag or pocket when folded

HOOKS AND LOOPS

Velcro™, which fastens things together quickly and easily, was invented in 1957 by a Swiss engineer, George de Mestral. He had examined burdock seeds under a microscope and seen how their tiny hooks clung to an animal's fur. He copied this idea to create Velcro™.

The design of Velcro™ means it can be used over and over again

A piece of Velcro™ is made up of two nylon strips, one covered with tiny hooks, the other with tiny loops

Hooks and loops bond tightly together but can be torn apart easily

Microsopic view of Velcro™

NEW GLUE

Post-it™ notes were invented by accident when an American company made a new glue. It didn't stick permanently and, at first, no one could see a use for the glue. But 11 years later, a choir singer, Arthur Fry, used it to make stickers to mark pages in his hymn book, showing how useful it could be.

Post-it™ notes can be stuck down, peeled off, and then restuck elsewhere

Some uses for Post-it™ notes

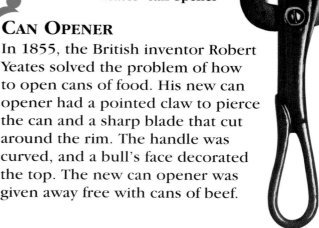

Yeates' can opener

CAN OPENER

In 1855, the British inventor Robert Yeates solved the problem of how to open cans of food. His new can opener had a pointed claw to pierce the can and a sharp blade that cut around the rim. The handle was curved, and a bull's face decorated the top. The new can opener was given away free with cans of beef.

Using Velcro™ in Space

PAPERCLIPS

Norwegian Johann Waaler invented the paperclip in 1900. He stopped other people from copying his idea by taking out a patent – a license giving only him the right to make and sell his paperclips for about 20 years.

Early paperclips

Ancient Egyptian clasp

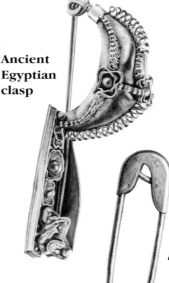

SAFETY PINS

In 1849, Charles Rowley and Walter Hunt invented the safety pin. Soon after, safety pins became widely available. Pins have a much longer history, though. Ancient Egyptians wore clasps to hold their clothing together. Inside each clasp was a pin. This idea inspired Rowley and Hunt to create the modern safety pin.

Modern safety pin

FIND OUT MORE

INSIDE MACHINES: Can opener
SPACE: Spacecraft

Clever Clothing

☞ Until the 20th century, most clothing was made from natural fibers, such as linen, cotton, or silk. In the 1930s, an artificial fiber called nylon was made. Since then, many different artificial fibers have been produced to make a variety of clothing. Artificial fibers make colorful everyday fabrics that are easy to care for. They also make tough outdoor clothing that keeps people warm in bad weather.

Waterproof clothing made from Gore-Tex®

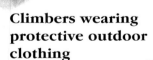

Elastic suspenders worn on pants

ELASTIC

When elastic first appeared in 1820, its English inventor Thomas Hancock used it on pockets to keep pickpockets' fingers out. Later, others saw how elastic would be much more useful for holding up pants and socks.

THERMAL FABRIC

Walkers, climbers, and sailors need clothing that keeps out the wind and rain. In 1976, an American chemist named Bill Gore developed Gore-Tex® from a kind of plastic. It is light, waterproof, and comfortable to wear, just right for outdoor activities.

Climbers wearing protective outdoor clothing

AMAZING FACTS

★ 2.5 cm² (1 square inch) of Gore-Tex® contains over 9 billion tiny holes. The holes are large enough to let sweat escape, but too small to let in the rain.

Plastic helmets are comfortably light, but protect the head if the climber falls

Thermal fabric gives protection from cold wind

Modern artificial dyes make bright colors that will not run or fade

Gloves lined with neoprene, a light, comfortable material that traps body heat

Boots are lightweight with thick treads for good grip

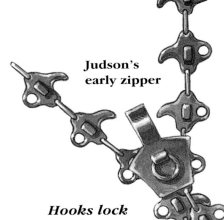

Judson's early zipper

Hooks lock together

ZIP UP

A zipper is quicker to open and close than a line of buttons. The first zipper was invented by an American engineer, Whitcomb Judson, in 1893. It was made of a long row of hooks and eyes, which were locked or unlocked by a slide. More than 20 years later, Gideon Sundback, a Swedish inventor, replaced the hooks with strong metal teeth.

BLUE JEANS

The American clothing manufacturer Levi Strauss made his first pair of denim jeans in the 1850s. At first, they were working clothes worn by gold miners. Today, Levi's uses 1.9 million km (1.2 million miles) of thread each year to make jeans – enough to go around the world 50 times.

Cowboys and cowgirl wearing denim jeans

Denim is a tough, hard-wearing fabric made from cotton

FIND OUT MORE
INSIDE MACHINES: Looms
SCIENCE ALL AROUND US: Technology

For the Body

☞ Having a clean, nice-smelling, attractive body is not a modern idea. Thousands of years ago, the Ancient Egyptians took showers, wore wigs and perfumes, and spent hours in front of their simple mirrors putting on exotic makeup. Today, modern technology provides us with many different ways of caring for our body. Electric toothbrushes and disposable razors are just some of the things we use to make us look and feel good.

CURLY HAIR

In 1906, a Swiss hairdresser named Karl Nestlé found a way of curling hair that lasted for several months. Until then, hairdressers had used heated tongs, but the hair needed re-curling every few days. The new "permanent" wave saved women a lot of time.

IN THE SHOWER

Archeologists working in Egypt believe that they have found the remains of showers that are 3,000 years old. The Ancient Greeks also washed in showers, as paintings on their pots clearly show.

Hair was divided *and rolled around electric curlers*

Each curler *was wrapped in folded paper containing a chemical called borax*

Small piece from a Greek vase painting, c. 500 B.C.

Borax set the hair *in a permanent wave, or "perm"*

Having a permanent wave, early 1900s

Hair stylists needed to be very skillful because the borax could burn the scalp and hair

CLEAN TEETH

Six hundred years ago, the people of China were using toothbrushes made from pig's hair to brush their teeth. Since then, the design of the toothbrush has hardly changed, although the bristles are now made of nylon. Electric toothbrushes were invented in 1908 and became popular after the 1930s.

Early electric toothbrush, 1950s

AMAZING FACTS

★ In ancient times, people cleaned their teeth using a handful of grass. Later, people made a kind of toothpaste from chalk and urine.

A CLOSE SHAVE

A hundred years ago, most men shaved with a cut-throat razor, which they had to sharpen often. In the early 1900s, an American salesman named King Camp Gillette invented a razor with a sharp steel blade that was replaced when it was blunt. It was one of the first disposable items, designed to be thrown away.

New blades are inserted safely from a dispenser

Safety covers hold the blade in place

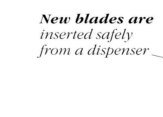

Gillette safety razor

Each blade has two cutting edges

FIND OUT MORE
HUMAN BODY: Hair
INSIDE MACHINES: Toothbrush

Medical Marvels

☞F or hundreds of years, people who needed surgery were usually terrified of what would happen to them. Patients were awake during operations and suffered dreadful pain, wounds often became infected, and many dangerous diseases could not be treated. Medical breakthroughs have led to anesthetics, antiseptics, and antibiotics – all of which are life-saving treatments.

SLEEPING SAFELY

Only 150 years ago, patients often died from pain and shock during operations. In 1846, an American dentist, William Morton, showed how a chemical called ether could put a patient safely to sleep for a short time, during which surgeons could operate. This reduced the number of patients who died from shock. It was the beginning of anesthetics.

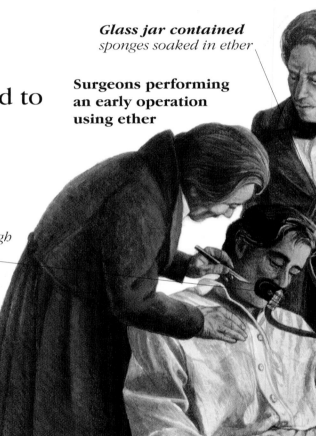

Glass jar contained *sponges soaked in ether*

Surgeons performing an early operation using ether

Patient breathed *in ether fumes through a mouthpiece*

LISTENING TO THE LUNGS

A French doctor called René Laënnec thought of the idea for a stethoscope when he saw children tapping messages to one another along a hollow piece of wood. In 1815, he made a simple wooden tube that helped him listen to his patients' chests.

Hollow wooden tube *made the sound of the lungs louder*

Early stethoscope, c. 1820s

Doctor listened *through the earpiece*

Surgeon worked *quickly while patient was asleep*

MEDICINE INJECTION

A hypodermic syringe injects medicines into the body through a sharp, hollow needle. Today's syringes use a plunger, but the first syringe, invented in 1853 by the French surgeon Charles Pravaz, had a handle that turned like a screw.

Early syringe, c. 1855

Handle
with screw

AMAZING FACTS

★ Before the use of anesthetics, surgeons had to work quickly. Some could amputate a leg in three minutes.

★ Without antiseptics, 50 patients out of every 100 died after an operation. When antiseptics were used, around 15 patients in 100 died.

LIFE-SAVING SPRAY

Many patients who survived operations died later of infection. In the 1870s, the British surgeon Joseph Lister used a steam kettle to spray carbolic acid in the air of the operating room and on his hands, gowns, bandages, and tools. This killed the germs that spread infection and was the start of modern antiseptics. Today, antiseptics are widely used in hospitals around the world.

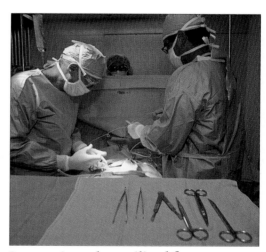

Surgeon's tools sterilized for use

Patient's pulse was
carefully checked
during the operation

FIND OUT MORE
GREAT LIVES: Medical pioneers
INSIDE MACHINES: Medical machines

Looking at Lenses

People have always been interested in seeing things more closely. Curved pieces of glass called lenses allow us to examine tiny objects in detail or see things that are far away. For hundreds of years, lenses have been used to correct people's sight. Glasses makers invented the microscope and telescope, which also use lenses. These instruments help scientists to observe and learn more about the world around us.

Lens and *eyepiece*

Hollow tube

Microscopes with two lenses are still called compound microscopes

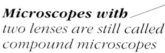

UNDER THE MICROSCOPE
The first microscope was a simple tube with a lens at each end. It was invented by a Dutch glasses maker named Hans Janssen in about 1590. Around 70 years later, a British inventor named Robert Hooke made an improved two-lens microscope that gave much clearer results.

Hooke's two-lens microscope

WEARING GLASSES
The first glasses were made in about 1280 by an Italian glassmaker named Salvano degli Amati. Two glass lenses were anchored in leather and held up to the eyes with a stick. If only one eye had poor vision, only one lens was needed. This was called a monocle.

First known illustration of a man wearing glasses, dated 1362

CONTACT LENSES

The first person to think of contact lenses was the Italian genius Leonardo da Vinci in the 1400s. About 200 years ago, astronomer John Herschel copied da Vinci's idea. He found he could see better after putting a layer of transparent gel on his eye.

Early contact lenses were made of thick glass

Lens — *Long tube with* *lens at each end*

Lens

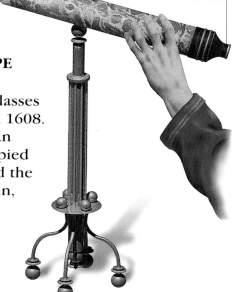

THROUGH A TELESCOPE

The first person to make a telescope was the Dutch glasses maker Hans Lippershey, in 1608. Three years later, the Italian scientist Galileo Galilei copied Lippershey's idea and used the telescope to look at the Sun, Moon, and planets.

Lippershey's telescope

Water in glass globe *focused the light of the flame onto the lens*

Light was bent by *the lens, making the image look bigger*

Flame provided *light source*

Oil for flame

Lens focused *light source*

Object or *specimen was placed on a pin*

AMAZING FACTS

★ About 2,500 years ago, the Ancient Greeks made magnifying glasses from glass globes filled with water.

FIND OUT MORE
SCIENCE ALL AROUND US: Lenses
SPACE: Telescopes

Photography

Photography was invented about 150 years ago. It must have seemed amazing that a camera could fix a moment in time forever. It was not long before people discovered that a fast-moving series of still pictures tricks the eye into thinking the images are moving. This is how the art of photography led to moviemaking, over a period of more than 50 years.

Taking a photo is easy today

Roll of camera film
safe in its cassette

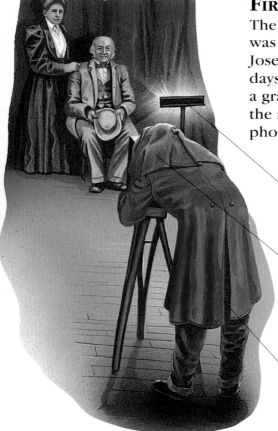

Early photography, c. 1880

FIRST PHOTOGRAPH

The world's first photograph was taken by the French inventor, Joseph Niepce, in 1826. In those days, it took eight hours before a grainy picture formed on the metal plate inside the photographer's camera.

Bright flash lit up *the sitters as the camera shutter opened*

Cloth was put *over the camera to protect the metal plate from light*

Photographer *focused image while sitters sat very still*

ON A ROLL

Early photography was a messy and complicated business using metal and glass plates and chemicals. In 1888, an American inventor named George Eastman developed camera film on a roll. Each time you took a photograph, you simply wound on the film. Film in modern cameras winds on automatically.

The first movies
showed anything
that moved

**Audience enjoying
a movie in Paris,
France, c. 1890s**

THE BIRTH OF MOVIES

In 1891, William Dickson
and Thomas Edison revealed
their kinetoscope – a device in
which a strip of film was passed
between a lens and a light bulb
to show a moving image. In 1895,
French brothers Auguste and Louis
Lumière developed a machine
called the Cinématographe, which
projected these moving images
onto a screen.

AMAZING FACTS

★ One of the first Lumière
films showed a train pulling
into a station. It was so
lifelike that some people
in the audience fainted for
fear they would be crushed.

The Cinématographe
was a film camera
and projector in one

FIND OUT MORE
COMMUNICATIONS: Movies
SCIENCE ALL AROUND US: Camera

Sound Recordings

Less than 100 years ago, the only way people could listen to music was to go to a concert and hear it being played. The invention of sound recording grew from the telephone. This inspired scientists to investigate ways of storing sounds. Thomas Edison led the way with the phonograph, but it was quickly followed by improved machinery that gave a much clearer sound.

RECORDING SOUND

In 1877, Thomas Edison invented a machine that could record a sound and play it back. He called it the phonograph. Although the recorded sound was not very clear, the machine was a breakthrough and inspired the invention of the gramophone.

Children listening to an early disk gramophone, c. 1906

Handle was turned as the person spoke into the horn

Edison's phonograph

CUTTING GROOVES

In 1888, a German-American scientist named Emile Berliner invented a machine that made a recording by cutting grooves in a flat disk. The disk was coated in a hard wax. Copies were made from this "master" disk. The copies were played on a gramophone, and the sound came through a metal horn. The sound quality was very good for the time.

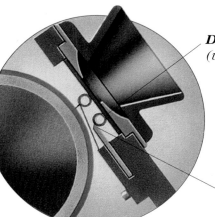

Diaphragm
(*vibrating disk*)

**Side view of
stylus working
on phonograph**

Vibrations from
*the diaphragm
touched a steel
needle (stylus)*

Horn directed
*sound waves
onto a diaphragm
(vibrating disk) with
a stylus attached*

Stylus pressed grooves
*into the tin foil wrapped
around drum, to make
the recording*

AMAZING FACTS

★ In 1903, a German
company produced a
chocolate disk. It was covered
with tin foil indented with
grooves. First you could play
it; then you could eat it.

MAGNETIC RECORDING

In 1898, a 20-year-old Danish
inventor, Valdemar Poulson,
made the first tape recorder.
His machine worked by changing
sound waves into patterns that
could be stored on magnetized
piano wire. When the wire was
wound past a magnet, the pattern
changed back into sounds. Forty
years later, the wire was replaced
by a light plastic tape.

Poulsen's magnetic recording machine

CDs TO TAKE WITH YOU

In 1982, two companies, Sony
and Philips, produced the
first compact disks (CDs).
Sounds were recorded in a
pattern of tiny pits on the
surface of the disk. These were
read by a laser beam and then
changed back into sounds.
Portable CD players have
been around since 1988.

**Portable compact
disk player**

FIND OUT MORE
GREAT LIVES: Thomas Alva Edison
INSIDE MACHINES: Music machines

FIND OUT MORE
GREAT LIVES: Thomas Alva Edison
INSIDE MACHINES: Music machines

Television and Radio

The invention of radio changed the world. For the first time, people could communicate over distances without being connected by wires. Guglielmo Marconi, the Italian inventor, started the radio revolution. He discovered how to send radio signals. Other inventors made further developments during the years that followed. Their skillful work led to the worldwide broadcasting industry that transmits, or sends out, news, information, and entertainment to millions of homes today.

Rotating disks with holes were placed in front of object being televised

Motor provided power to turn the disks

FIRST TELEVISION

Television was invented in 1925 by a Scottish scientist named John Logie Baird. His working model was made from odd bits and pieces, including a hatbox lid, a knitting needle, a bicycle lamp, and an electric fan. The first picture transmitted, or sent out, was of a blurred human face.

Baird's television transmitting picture of a puppet's face

AMAZING FACTS

★ The wind-up radio was invented in the early 1990s. It is perfect for people in faraway parts of the world because it does not need batteries or electricity. Winding it up for 30 seconds keeps it going for about an hour.

Wind-up radio, invented by Trevor Bayliss

Light passed *through holes in the disks*

Puppet's head *to be televised*

WIRELESS

Guglielmo Marconi was only 20 years old when he found a way to transmit radio signals. Working in his attic, in 1894, he succeeded in sending messages across the room by using invisible electrical waves. Seven years later, he was able to send radio signals halfway around the world.

Marconi sending out a message over the radio

VIDEOS

Video tape was invented by the Russian engineer Alexander Pontiatoff in 1956. The magnetic tape saved sounds and pictures in the form of electrical signals. The first video recorders were used by television stations. By 1975, the machines were cheap and simple enough to use in the home.

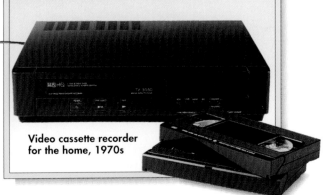

Video cassette recorder for the home, 1970s

TINY TRANSISTOR

The first transistor radios appeared in the U.S. in 1954. They were named after new electronic devices, called transistors, that boosted the tiny electrical signals received by the set. Transistors were small and could be powered by batteries. This led to the invention of smaller electronic machines.

Handheld transistor, 1950s

FIND OUT MORE
COMMUNICATIONS: Radio
INSIDE MACHINES: Television

Computers

Computers as we know them first appeared about 50 years ago, and are the most important recent invention. Early computers were huge and unreliable, but the invention of transistors led to smaller, more useful machines. By the 1960s, scientists had found a way to store transistors and other electronic components on silicon chips measuring just 5 mm (¼ in) square. Modern computers are used at home and at work, for playing games, running complex machines, and even operating satellites in Space.

MECHANICAL COMPUTER

In 1834, Charles Babbage, a British mathematician, began building a mechanical computer. It was as big as a large bus and contained 50,000 gears, levers, and rods that were to be driven by steam. The machine was never completed, but the idea was many years ahead of its time.

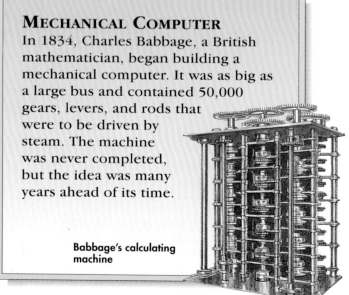

Babbage's calculating machine

THE COMPUTER AGE

Modern computing began with the Electronic Numeral Integrator And Calculator, or ENIAC. It was built in the U.S. in 1946 by John Mauchly and John Eckert. It weighed as much as 30 cars and filled a whole room. It could perform fewer tasks than a modern programable calculator.

ENIAC was programed by plugging in wires and throwing switches

AMAZING FACTS

★ Computers that once filled entire rooms can now be made small enough to fit on your lap.

Steven Jobs, John Scully, and Stephen Wozniak
of Apple Computer Company

APPLE II

Americans Steven Jobs and
Stephen Wozniak founded the
Apple Computer Company in
a garage in 1976. In 1978, they
launched the Apple II, the first
personal computer that was
popular in the West and easy
to use. The computer was
sold along with a keyboard.

**The first floppy disks
got their name
because they
were bendy**

*Instructions were
stored electronically in
the computer's memory*

Built before the invention
of the transistor, ENIAC had
19,000 valves to control the
flow of electricity

**Technicians checking
ENIAC's controls**

IBM FLOPPY DISK
The floppy disk, invented in
1950 in Japan, was a handy
way to store computer
information. It became
very popular after the
launch of the first personal
computers (PCs).

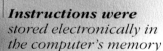

FIND OUT MORE
COMMUNICATIONS: Computers
INSIDE MACHINES: Computers

Living with Inventions

When inventors develop a new idea, they hope it will make people's lives easier. But no inventor can predict the future. While many inventions change our lives for the better, some are simply failures and others bring new problems.

Cars are useful, but increasing use of them has led to all kinds of problems: air pollution, more accidents, and crowded roads. The challenge for today's inventors is to find new ways of saving energy and reducing waste. Cleaner cars and environment-friendly products, such as recyclable containers and cleaning fluids with less harmful chemicals, are a good start.

Bottles ready to be picked up for recycling

KIND TO THE ENVIRONMENT

Household waste includes materials such as glass, plastic, and metal. When it is thrown away it creates ugly garbage dumps and causes pollution because it does not rot. Machines can sort waste and recycle it into new materials. This saves energy and resources, and helps the environment.

Used bottles, cans, cartons, and plastic containers from the home can be sorted for recycling, and other household waste put out for disposal

Some containers made from recycled materials may have been in the home before

Useful garbage is taken away and recycled

Recyclable waste can be made into new containers, saving energy and basic materials

Most garbage is buried in huge holes called landfill sites, which can spoil the environment

CFC-FREE AEROSOLS

Aerosols contain gases that change their liquid contents into a spray. Scientists discovered that some of these gases (known as CFCs) were damaging the ozone layer of the Earth's atmosphere, letting in harmful ultraviolet rays from the Sun. Manufacturers are now using fewer harmful gases, or making pump-action sprays with no gases in them at all.

Pump-action spray

Aerosol spray

CLEAN CAT

Removing poisonous lead additives from gas has made exhaust fumes less harmful. Modern cars are also fitted with a catalytic converter, or "cat," which converts unburned fuel and exhaust fumes into water vapour and non-poisonous carbon dioxide.

Non-recyclable garbage is collected and taken to a dumping ground

Car being filled with lead-free gas, which makes less harmful exhaust fumes

GREEN CLEAN
Washing machines save time and effort, but use up a lot of electricity and water. Manufacturers are now producing machines that use less of both. Scientists are developing better washing powders that do not pollute the environment.

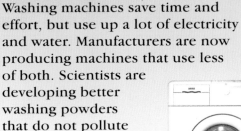

Modern washing machines are more environment-friendly

Waste disposal and recycling

FIND OUT MORE
PLANET EARTH: Environmental issues
SCIENCE ALL AROUND US: Technology

Glossary of Key Words

Amplify: To make louder.

Anesthetic: A substance that is given to a patient before an operation so that he or she will not feel pain.

Antibiotic: A medicine that can help to cure some illnesses by killing harmful germs.

Antiseptic: A substance, usually a liquid or cream, that prevents infection when applied to skin.

Archeologist: A person who finds out how people used to live by examining objects that they left behind.

Astronomer: A scientist who studies moving objects in Space.

Biodegradable: Able to be broken down naturally, by bacteria or other living things, when left in the ground.

Broadcasting: Transmitting, or sending out radio waves that carry radio or television programs.

Detergent: A chemical product used to clean such things as dishes and clothes.

Diaphragm: In microphones or loudspeakers, a thin piece of plastic, metal, or paper that vibrates to pick up or make sound.

Dynamo: A machine that produces electricity from movement.

Energy: The ability to make things move or work. Energy comes from such things as the Sun, fuels, and the movement of water and wind.

Engine: A machine that changes heat into energy.

Engineering: Designing and making things such as machines, buildings, and bridges.

Evaporation: When a liquid turns into a gas.

Fertilizer: A substance that is added to the soil to make plants grow faster and bigger.

Fiber: A thin thread. In fabrics, cotton is a natural fiber and nylon is an artificial, or man-made, fiber.

Flywheel: A wheel with a heavy rim that keeps a machine moving smoothly as it turns.

Fuel: A substance, such as gasoline, that burns to make heat or power.

Furnace: A very hot oven. Furnaces have many uses, such as for melting metals and baking clay.

Laser: A special light source that produces a narrow, bright, and powerful beam of light.

Lens: A piece of transparent material with one or more curved surfaces that bend light to produce an image, or picture.

Magnet: A magnet produces forces that can attract or repel (pull toward or push away) another magnet. Magnets also attract things made of iron.

Magnetized: Made into a magnet.

Mass-produce: To make a product in large numbers using machines.

Material: The substance from which an object is made. Also meaning "fabric."

Mechanical motion: Movement of a machine or movement produced by a machine.

Microscope: An instrument containing one or more lenses that makes very small things look large enough for the eye to see.

Mold: A hollow, shaped container that is used to give a shape to melted solids as they cool and set.

Oil refinery: A factory where oil from under the ground is separated into different substances, including gasoline and diesel.

Patent: The recorded right of an inventor to claim and use an idea as his or her own.

Photoelectric cell: A device that turns light energy into electricity.

Plate: A flat, thin piece of metal or glass.

Propeller: A set of spinning blades that push a ship through the water or pull some types of airplanes through the air.

Research laboratory: A place where scientists, engineers, and mechanics investigate and solve problems, and develop new ideas.

Safety standard: A set of rules against which people can measure how safe things are.

Silicon chip: A small piece of a material called a semiconductor containing thousands or millions of transistors or other electric components.

Technology: The use of science to solve problems or make things.

Telescope: An instrument with lenses used to make faraway objects seem closer.

Transistor: An electronic component, or part, inside radios and other machines that "reads" electrical signals.

Voltage: A measurement, in units known as volts, used in electric circuits and batteries.

Index

*(see **Famous Places** for a full index to your complete set of books)*